£2.
8~

Grace Publishing is an independent company founded on a 'not for profit' basis, dedicated to publishing material of general interest but which points to a meaning and significance to life beyond that which is immediately apparent in our postmodern society.

Further details can be obtained at www.gracepublishing.co.uk or by writing to:

Grace Publishing Ltd.

The Stone House
123 High Street
Henley-in-Arden
Warwickshire
B95 5AU.

A Candle on Kilimanjaro

The story of a trek

The Author

Born at Solihull in 1960, James Holden has worked as a Public Relations consultant for most of his adult life. He read history at Sheffield University and, after a spell in London, found himself back in Birmingham at the advertising agency his father established in 1965.

James has three children and lives in Henley-in-Arden, a picturesque market town to the north of Stratford-upon-Avon. He is currently taking a Diploma in Biblical and Theological Studies at Wycliffe Hall, Oxford.

The Designer

Kevin Roberts is a Black Countryman born and bred and lives in Dudley – the unofficial capital of a part of the West Midlands renowned as the cradle of the industrial revolution. Kevin has wide experience in the world of advertising and design and has worked on some of the world's best-known brands. He is married to Andrea and has three children.

James Holden

A Candle on Kilimanjaro

The story of a trek

grace
publishing

This edition published in Great Britain in 2002 by

Grace Publishing Ltd
The Stone House
123 High Street
Henley in Arden
Warwickshire B95 5AU

Cover illustration: Mawenzi from the peak of Kibo at daybreak. 24 June 2001

A CIP catalogue record for this book is available from the British Library.

ISBN: 0954198204 Cloth bound edition.
ISBN: 0954198212 Paperback edition.

Art Direction: Kevin Roberts
Designed and typeset by Leader Communications Ltd
Henley-in-Arden, Warwickshire.

Printed and bound in Great Britain

For Barbara

Introduction

Photo: ST

The word 'challenge' does not always enjoy priority in our vocabulary today. In times characterised by the 'settle for' mentality, there is a preference for life experiences that do not create too much disturbance and disruption. Stimulation of body, mind and soul does not always appear to enjoy a measure of importance.

The Trailblazers programme, initiated by the Saltmine Trust, is an innovative attempt to introduce people from all walks of life, to the thrills of rising to personal, physical and spiritual challenge. It is more than an exercise in 'doing something different' or fulfilling personal dreams and ambitions; it is an opportunity to push boundaries, to explore the dynamics of team work, to be 'Christ' in the real world and to make a significant difference through the respect and responsible use of financial resources.

James' testimony is not untypical of those who have been involved in a Trailblazers' challenge, although his creativity, flair and expression are exceptional. But just as he was able to apply his faith in a practical way, so that challenge exists for all of us who take issues of belief and commitment seriously.

Enjoy the book, but don't forget to look beyond the printed page!

Dave Pope
Chairman: Saltmine Trust
West Midlands – March 2002

Foreword

It is my hope that reading this book may focus your mind on areas not previously considered. I can assure you that for all those who undertook this expedition it was a significant spiritual and emotional experience.

As a team we are unanimous in our gratitude to James, who through his skill and ability has transferred the experience of his trek into the words and pictures that comprise: 'A Candle on Kilimanjaro'. We too shared many of these experiences and it is good that they are now available to all.

We started with a single goal – to conquer Kibo, the awe-inspiring summit of Mount Kilimanjaro. We had just one thing in common – our faith. The next few days were to deepen that faith, consolidate and develop our skills, test us and virtually drain us of all our physical and emotional strength. Most importantly, however, our trek would enlighten our personal spiritual growth.

Everyone I have met who has taken on the challenge of this mountain has said that to climb 'Kili' was one of the most incredible feats of their lives. Having been there, I can only concur with those sentiments.

I trust that in reading this book you will acknowledge and capture the awesome splendour of God's magnificent creation. Who knows, you too may also find yourself as 'A Candle on Kilimanjaro' one day!

Mike Freeman, MBE

Saltmine Kilimanjaro 2001 Team Leader

MOUNT KILIMANJARO—TANZANIA

SUMMIT — 5895 m.
Gillman's point 5685 m.

This is to Certify that

Mr./Mrs./Miss *JAMES   HOLDEN*

has successfully climbed Mount Kilimanjaro
the highest peak in Africa, right to the
Summit - Uhuru Peak - 5895 m.

Date *2A^th JUNE 200* Time *6:30 Am* Age *41*

Joachim . P. MTUI
GUIDE

PARK WARDEN
Mt. Kilimanjaro National Park

DIRECTOR GENERAL
Tanzania National Parks

CERTIFICATE No. *17042/0,*

Acknowledgements

There are so many people to thank and recognise for their help and support on the trek and in the production of this book. Often though, I have found it a dangerous business to thank people by name, for fear of forgetting someone and causing more hurt than pleasure. It needs to be recorded that 'A Candle on Kilimanjaro' was inspired (at least in part) by a speech given by Julius Nyerere on 22nd October 1959 to the Tanganyika Legislative Assembly. That speech emphasised the demand that majority self-government should replace British colonial rule. Others are better placed to judge whether independence has been a success for Tanzania, but for me light and hope come from a quite different source.

Specifically though, thanks are due to my sponsors and subscribers for their generosity; to my staff for their long forbearance; to friends, clients and family; to the people who have commented on the text (but for which I take sole responsibility); to fellow trekkers and lastly our guides and porters without whose support and strength I'd still be labouring up the mountain.

The effort will have been worthwhile if readers are challenged and encouraged to find the true source of light in their lives.

Henley -in-Arden

12th February 2002

How Kilimanjaro got on my wick

I really don't know how it happened. How I came to be driving down this dirt track in Tanzania in a beat-up old bus. It's pitch black and sticky hot. On the side of the road there are what look like wooden huts, only if they were in your garden at home you'd pull them down and put up new ones. They're falling to pieces and not one of them looks like it's been erected straight. Occasionally one of them has a light in it and through the open door I can see black faces swigging from bottles. I guess they're pubs, Tanzanian style.

The track leads up a steady slope and suddenly we pass through some gates onto a smooth metalled driveway. I can see the flash of white teeth illuminated by light flooding through the glass windows of a swanky safari lodge. The bus comes to a stop. Our gear is hefted off the roof rack and the white teeth swarm towards us to porter our climbing gear into the lodge. I jog in as quickly as possible since I've been told the malaria tablets I'm on aren't any use in Tanzania, and there are 'zillions of mozzies' buzzing round the lights leading up to our lodge.

The funny thing is that it all started when I was in this tent with thousands of people at Butlins. It was a bit like the sort of thing you sit in at the circus only much bigger. This rather rugged bloke called Nick - he looked a real explorer type by the way - was introducing an adventure called the Biscay Challenge. It sounded great:

'A crew of 12 volunteers will embark on a 1,400 nautical mile journey on a 67ft Global Challenge yacht under the instruction of a professional skipper. No previous sailing experience is required, but after training every crew member will be hands on – helming, rigging and adjusting the sails.'

I fell hook line and sinker for the idea when Nick showed us a wide-screen video of a gorgeous boat cutting through the ocean with consummate ease. He told of how dolphins followed in its wake, of horizons without limit. I went straight round to Nick's display unit in the foyer afterwards and signed up to climb all 19,455 feet of Kilimanjaro! At times I've had doubts about my sanity. Right now I'm absolutely convinced that I'd be great company for the Mad Hatter himself!

Instead of cruising around the Bay of Biscay I'm about to face a flog up an extinct volcano and all because too many people got to Nick ahead of me. What a pity I wasn't motivated by a 'zillion mozzies' to jog a bit faster when I was at Butlins. Right now we're in the lounge at the lodge drinking freshly squeezed passion fruit juice and chomping on hot toasties. We British-based climbers – there are ten of us – have just been joined by four Zimbabweans and our leaders are running through the itinerary for the next couple of days. Even though I'm feeling quite comfy right now I'm still trying to answer the nagging question of why I'm here. Everyone else seems to be so much better prepared for the ordeal that's in front of us. You know, I really don't want to be climbing Kilimanjaro. I'd be much happier supping a pint of Guinness Extra Cold back home in 'The Bluebell' with maybe a Chicken Balti carry-out from the Arden Tandoori to fill up any lingering holes.

I'm acutely aware that my training programme for the challenge has been pitiful. The other climbers seem to have been preparing for months and months. The boys from 'Zim' have trained particularly rigorously and most of the British climbers have been working out in the gym and running and swimming regularly. Even the one or two that don't seem to have prepared too well are about two decades younger than me. My own training has been woeful. I've played a few sets of tennis at my local club, helped a friend dig over her potato patch one Sunday afternoon and I did a fun run in Sutton Park, just north of Birmingham, a couple of weeks before leaving for Africa.

An old university mate of mine asked me round to his house for the weekend : 'Come round and relax for the weekend,' he'd promised 'and on the Sunday why not join me and a few of the lads from our rugby club on the Sutton Fun Run? Go on Jim, It'll be a laugh.' Well it was never a laugh, but at least at first it was fun. I'd set off at a briskish pace with one of the rugger-muckers and for four miles everything was fine. The weather was lovely – warm and sunny with a slight breeze. There was a big crowd lining the way and they were very encouraging.

Suddenly, just before the halfway point, my legs began to feel a little stiff. By the time I reached the next drinks' table I had to stop running just to check that there wasn't a serious problem with my left knee. After that I didn't break above a limping amble for the rest of the run. In fact, it wasn't a run anymore and it certainly wasn't any fun. My legs went agonisingly stiff. They were like a pair of cocktail sticks that simply wouldn't bend. I wasn't tired or out of breath, mind you: I couldn't go fast enough to put myself in any danger of that! The thought flashed through my mind that I must be the only person whose assault on Kilimanjaro had been thwarted in Sutton Park. I didn't need to worry about Malaria or Yellow Fever or altitude sickness – a jog in the park was enough to finish me off.

And yet here I am, here in Tanzania, in the third world, for the first time in my life - about to climb the highest point in all Africa. A peak that was scaled for the first time in 1889 by a couple of top German climbers. They named the conquered summit after their ruler - 'Kaiser Wilhelm Spitze'. It's now called Uhuru peak since Tanzania has escaped the yoke of colonialism. If you don't already know (and really there's no particular reason why you should) Uhuru is Swahili for freedom, which I find quite alluring as I've always rather liked Lieutenant Uhuru in 'Star Trek.' I shall always think of her as Lieutenant Freedom now – nice thought that!

Right now, I'm taking a shower. I'm sharing a room with this guy from Northern Ireland. He's a decent sort of bloke

- about the same age as me. I think he has some of the same concerns about why he's on the trip, but he's certainly trained more assiduously than I have and he's raised an awful lot more sponsorship money. The water's cold, which is a bit of a shock given that we're only a few miles south of the equator. But in a way I'm glad - it's quite refreshing after a full day's travelling.

The rooms are nice though, even down to having mosquito nets festooned over the beds, like giant spiders' webs: very reassuring when your malaria pills don't work. My bags were carried to my room by a smartly-dressed African woman - all the hotel porters seem to be women. On reflection I'm not all that happy about having my rucksack carried for me. Maybe it's because I'm not sure how the tipping system works or maybe I'm just an archaic chauvinist. Either way, watching a slender woman bending double under the weight of a load of climbing gear was not something I found particularly edifying.

Whilst I towel myself off I nearly make the mistake of pouring myself a glass of water. I'm really thirsty and physical need makes me forget the strict instructions we've received about not drinking the water. Fortunately, in the bathroom cabinet there's a bottle of treated water with a picture of Kilimanjaro on it. I check the label first and feel a surge of confidence when I read that Kilimanjaro-branded water is absolutely pure, thanks to the use of the latest Swiss filtration technology in its production. Thank heavens for the Swiss! My room mate wants a shower, so I must finish drying myself, vacate the bathroom and go through to the bedroom to get my things ready for tomorrow and prepare myself for sleep.

After a bit of a fumble with the mosquito net I manage to get comfortable, although with only one blanket I've got to say that I do feel a bit chilly. I'm starting to think about the subject of sponsorship. As I said earlier, the Irish guy's raised a lot of money. I thought I'd done well and indeed my family, friends and colleagues have been really generous, but he's put me in the shade. I'm doing the climb in aid of a charity called the Saltmine Trust. It's a really worthwhile organisation and one of the ways it supports its activities is through people like us taking on sponsored challenges. We have had to cover our own costs and make a donation to the charity ourselves and then each of us has had to encourage as many people as possible to 'dig deep'. I found doing that really embarrassing, but somehow I did manage to ask people and they were mostly very sympathetic. It was quite amazing how one man I'd never met got a sponsorship form from his father-in-law (whom I knew only slightly) and felt compelled to start raising funds by asking all his work colleagues for their support. I think it's fair to say that charity is one of the main reasons I've given to others for wanting to climb Kili. At least it's one that people understand without questioning your sanity!

As I lie awake in the darkness I'm disturbed by a sudden loud howl. It's a long, low noise that seems to last for minutes although it's probably only a matter of seconds. As the howl dies down another follows, then another, then another…. until my ears are assailed by a cacophony of unbroken howling. It seems that every dog in the district has suddenly found its voice and is giving full vent at the moon that I had spied whilst we travelled down the dirt track to this little oasis of western luxury in the desert. It's a foreboding sound, a bit like the rather scary (but somewhat ludicrous) noise they use to signal the presence of the demon dog in the Hound of the Baskervilles in plays and films.

I'm struck by the sobering thought that in the morning our challenge will begin. That we'll get our first look at the great mountain rising dramatically from the flat plain and that I'll begin to find out much more about what my fellow climbers are like. From what I've read the likelihood is that at least 5 or 6 of us should fail; although Saltmine's never had a failure yet because the long and gradual ascent route they use minimises the likelihood of altitude sickness striking. I reckon everyone's got me earmarked as the one most likely to fail.

Whilst on the subject of failure I call to mind my birthday party that I'd held just a week or so before departure. It was a joint party with a friend who works at my company. Funny that in all my years she's the only person I've ever met with the same birthday as me! It was a pig roast held in her parent's huge garden. In fact their garden's so big that it's really more of a field than a garden. I remember that a number of people at the party asked me why I was going to try and climb Kilimanjaro. I trotted out some of my usual answers in between mouthfuls of pork bap laden with apple sauce and stuffing: 'For charity'; 'Because it's there'; 'Because I need to test myself and find out whether I'm up for it'.

Now, as the howls die down, I realise that I still don't really know the answer. I think it's got something to do with finding out, with seeking, with wanting to know the answer to a question that I hardly dare to formulate. A question which something tells me we all of us ask at some point in our lives. That same something tells me that the problem is we don't listen for the answer which always seems to be whispered to us whenever we pose the question.

Of a sudden I recall a funny thing that happened at the end of my party. My father had driven my eldest son back to the school where he weekly boards and I had put some of his things into the car boot. When my other children were ready to go home my daughter found that she hadn't got her school-things. We reckoned I must have put them in dad's car by mistake and hoped against hope that he hadn't dropped them off with my son.

When I got home I phoned dad. "Have you got Beth's school things in your car?" I asked. "No, I'm sure I haven't," came the reply, "but I'll just take you out to the car while I check."

Silence and a bit of a crackle as he took his cordless phone out onto the driveway....

"I'm at the car now" (sound of boot lid springing open). "No! nothing here, and nothing in the car either. I know I haven't got them. What are you going to do now?"

A very good question I thought to myself, as I contemplated a distraught daughter. "Let me know if it turns up", concluded dad: "Bye now."

The bag must have been left at the party – surely! I phoned-up my fellow celebrant. A curse on answering machines! I'll have to drive up to the garden and look for it. I pulled up, went through the back gate and saw that a few party-goers were still there polishing off the dregs. I hadn't wanted them to see my error but I aped cheerfulness and told them about the lost bag. There was widespread sympathy when they heard my tale but there seemed little enthusiasm to help me search the pitch-black field. It looked hopeless and I felt a surge of desperation – funny isn't it how little things can take on gigantic proportions? And then, just when all seemed lost, there it was on the chair by the pig roast basking in a pool of light; exactly where we must have put it down when she arrived. What a surge of relief! Odd that, the thing that was lost being sought for everywhere, whilst all the time it's where you first put it down - just waiting for you to find it.

I'm really rather tired right now. There's still the occasional howl to disturb but it's relatively peaceful and I've been up since four this morning. From a Black Country flat near the Saltmine offices in Dudley to a safari lodge on the Dark Continent in less than 24 hours – not bad eh! I'm very aware that I still don't really understand why I'm here. Does it matter? Not really, I suppose, it's just that it keeps niggling at me. As I doze off a picture comes into my semi-consciousness. It's of an English wood in spring. It's mid-May and the bluebells are out. They're a shade of blue that defies description.

A well-wisher gave me a little good luck card before I left that had a picture of bluebells on it, just like the one I've got in my head. It's a picture that reminds me of woods I walked in my salad days. Inside the card there's a quotation from the Book of Ecclesiastes:

'There is a time for everything,
And a season for every activity under heaven.
A time to love,
And a time to hate
A time of war
And a time of peace.'

(Ecc 3:1 and 8)

I find that very reassuring, but right now all that I really want is some kip. Those dogs are still at it, why won't they just shut up? Whatever, sleep continues to elude me. Let's put it down to a growing impatience for daybreak so that I can see the challenge ahead.

Photo: JC

A Candle on Kilimanjaro

I

A cruel coming we had of it
And a cruel going.

Aeons ago the plain had buckled,
Slipped and fractured.
Molten lava spewed through
Great rents in the crust.
The plains stretched as paddyfields of rust
Pockmarked by volcanoes.
Three peaks – Shira, Mawenzi and Kibo –
Rose ever higher from those fields.

A Candle on Kilimanjaro

Higher and higher they grew
Spewing forth elemental rock
And gas and fire till each in turn abated.
First Shira became a caldera.
Then jagged toothed Mawenzi died.
Only Kibo the young giant grew
Till finally the mountain cooled,
Slumbered and crouched under ice and snow
Remote and unconquered.

Is a mountain to be conquered? Many said yes!
But isn't it more about realising a dream?
In colonial times Tanganyika groaned,
Cried out for freedom and saw the light on Kibo:

'We would like to light a candle and put it on top of
Kilimanjaro which would shine beyond our borders,
give hope where there was despair, love where there
was hate and dignity where before there was only humiliation.'

A Candle on Kilimanjaro

Photo: JC

Did we come to conquer,
Or did we come to see the light?
It was a cruel coming
And a cruel going
But there was a light
And some did see.

A Candle on Kilimanjaro

II

No man can tame his tongue
For it drips with deadly poison.
Yet I shall try to tell a
Full and unvarnished tale
Of how we conquered mighty Kibo.
And yet in our conquering
Admit that to succeed
We had first to fail.

A Candle on Kilimanjaro

That whatever appeared so
Was not necessarily so;
Yet whatever was so
Our labour was not in vain.

Certainly we came to conquer
But it was better to see the light.
It was a cruel coming
And crueller going away.

III

We approached the mountain
Through the quilted plain.
Planted at first with fruit and grain
Ever wilder, ever drier it became.

A jackal slunk away toward a
Herd of gazelle and soon our camp was in view.

A place of plenty
Of food, of fellowship, of comfort
Of calm before the storm.
A place for us to increase
Before we must decrease.
A first training walk
Safari like on the flat lulled us.

Photo: JC

A Candle on Kilimanjaro

And tuskers bathing and spied
With baboon and impala from a tree hide,
Took our minds away from what we saw
Rising ahead like a mirage.
Kilimanjaro beckoned in challenge.
We huddled that night round a fire
And told brave stories of how we'd prepared.

It was easy so far.
But the ease served only to make
The cruel seem crueller.

Photo: CF

A Candle on Kilimanjaro

IV

We bumped along the mountain road 4x4
Past villages, crops and herdsmen;
Carrots, cabbages and beans
Grew in fields recently felled
In soil rich and red.
Whilst passports were checked at the gate
Smiling children from a shanty
Of split logs and tarpaulin gathered round.

A Candle on Kilimanjaro

Photo: CF

'Jambo bwana' they cried
From dirty American 'T' shirts.
At first sight all seemed healthy and happy
But whatever appeared so
Was not necessarily so.
As they drank from my pack
One boy hung back
Then stoppered the tube and pointed
To greyish faces 1 in 4.

Photo: JC

A Candle on Kilimanjaro

We could sense the plague,
We could see it,
And they could touch us, wanted to touch us
They did touch us and though we were not infected
All were touched.
None would be the same again.
None could be the same again.

It was getting harder you see.
Was Kibo the cruellest thing we had to scale?

V

In earnest we began to walk
Through a damp, foggy forest
Of strange trees and ferns
Of orchids and balsam.
Branches encrusted with lichens and moss,
Festooned with creepers and hanging things
Seeking light and water.
Only occasionally a shaft of light
Penetrated the gloom.
But as we went higher the
Light grew stronger
The trees thinner.

A Candle on Kilimanjaro

Metallic butterflies flitted past.
Turacos and hornbills cried in the canopy
And a group of monkeys spoke unseen.
On and on we went,
Up and up we went
Till we reached a clearing
Where porters had pitched the tents.
We were of good courage.
It was not so cruel,
Until we recalled the children
Then it was chill in my bag.

VI

The sun dispelled the chill,
The trees petered out
And we were in a different land:
A heath that stretched
East to west
North to south
Across the vast expanse of Shira.
What once had been a mighty peak
Had collapsed and now was flat.

A Candle on Kilimanjaro

The way went on
And on
And on
For mile after mile across the flat.
The sun tired, the clouds gathered
Low and cool,
Gusting in wisps,
Collecting in hollows.
And we were tired.
Dog tired.
Exhausted I sat alone to hear
The sound of silence;

A Candle on Kilimanjaro

It lay all around
In a colourless world.
Yet suddenly, unexpectedly
The sun re-emerged
And dappled the land again
With substance and shadow.
A raven called as if to say:
'Follow me. Return to your tent.'

It was a hard coming that day.

VII

In every challenge,
In every life there are those moments
Those defining moments
When giving up seems easier than going on.
Yet somehow, intuitively
From deep within,
From the heart's core
Something drives us on.
That day my head hammered.
My guts were on fire.
The altitude sickened me.

Photo: JC

A Candle on Kilimanjaro

Every sinew cried out:
'Enough, enough it is finished'.
Shira Cathedral towered above
A remnant of the collapsed rim.
I had to go up,
I had to go up….
I did go up, and down and on.

But it was a cruel coming
And a cruel going
And it was twilight when we arrived.

A Candle on Kilimanjaro

VIII

It was cold,
Bitter cold.
The porters were refractory
Cursing and grumbling in Swahili.
Light snow turned to a squall,
The squall to a storm.
As we scaled new heights
I regretted the time on the plain.
The warmth,
The beer,
The bonhomie,
My warm bed,
It was no training for this.
A lunchtime bivouac collapsed
Its shelter destroyed by snow.

A Candle on Kilimanjaro

We shivered – cold and wet,
But when we descended
The snow melted to rain.
Warm driving rain.
Sweet smell of vegetation in a green valley;
The gurgling of a newly fed stream.

Still it was a bitter, sore-footed day
And a damp night.

IX

A 100,000 years ago
A landslide sliced a chunk off Kibo's summit.
As the sun dried us,
Our kit and restored the porters' humour
We surveyed the result of the wounding –
The great Barranco breach wall.
It was sheer. The only way up was
'Pole , pole' – 'slowly slowly'–
Our watchword henceforth
As we snaked up the gash
One slip and….
It was a long way down.

Photo: JC

A Candle on Kilimanjaro

We pursued some Americans,
And caught them at the top
And then we plunged down
Whilst they went up.
Some called their families from the peak.
I felt sad, deeply sad
But then words came to me
'Pole, pole
Pursue , overtake, recover all.
I arrived dead on my feet –
Slept without supper
Fitfully till dawn.

How many sorts of cruelty are there?

Photo: JC

X

Be strong and don't give up,
Don't quit
Even though the vegetation has.
It's a desert today as far as the eye can see.
The sun's hot,
The ground is dry and sharp.
Below us the clouds are rolling away
Like an endless sea.

A Lammergeier floats into view
Riding the thermals effortlessly on stiff wings.
We toil on stiffening legs towards our last high camp.
The Americans come past us
They made it but they look ill.
Tired, they say it's great
But their looks disagree.

The vulture suddenly drops from view.
Will our work be rewarded
Or is it all to be in vain?

It was easy today.
Tomorrow we summit – or not.

A Candle on Kilimanjaro

XI

We're awoken before midnight
Head torch on.
Pitch black.
The African sky illuminated by the brightest stars
The milky way slips away from left to right.
But the way is hard
Really hard.
All that has gone before is easy
Really easy.
Someone keels over but is revived.

Someone turns back.
The group splits up.
Those ahead have help
Those behind have guides
We in the middle are alone
Middle aged, in the middle and alone.
An hour before dawn one man yells
Oh God why am I here'?
Another hesitates and slips on the scree.
It's so, so steep and no one to help us –
Abandoned and no light.

A Candle on Kilimanjaro

Wait a torch light,
A voice: 'Just another ten yards and you're up.'
It's not the peak but the rest is easy.
Uhuru peak by sunrise and all Africa before us.

A Candle on Kilimanjaro

The light plays on the glaciers,
Colours the sky with a vivid palette.
Cold yes, freezing yes, pleased yes,
But there's still the coming down.
Kibo is not beaten
But the dream is realised.
Darkness nearly crushed the light,
But light burns as well as shines
And strangely going on
Was easier than giving up.

XII

A hard and cruel time we had of it.
And I asked God why?
He didn't say directly.
Yet the final assault called to mind a different hill –
Climbed by another –
Another who died and rose to light the world.
Certainly a part of me has died
Has been crucified.

A Candle on Kilimanjaro

Surely the light I saw on Kibo
Will pierce the gloom,
Will bring hope where there is despair,
Love where there is hate,
Dignity where now there is humiliation.

I should be glad of another coming.

A Guttering Candle

It's nearly a year since I climbed mighty Kibo and I'm making my way towards a pub at Butlins, in Skegness. I'm going to meet this guy called Mark who climbed the mountain with me. He was the one in the poem who told me I'd only got ten yards to go. I bumped into him at the swimming pool earlier today just before I joined the queue for the 'Master Blaster'. Great ride the 'Master Blaster'. You get into an inflated raft and then this attendant pushes you towards a gaping hole and .... *whoosh!* you disappear into a perpendicular tube which then snakes a roller-coaster course for hundreds of yards.

I'm walking along this wide avenue past the pool and up towards the pub where we'd agreed to meet. I guess you've seen the old posters featuring the slogan 'Skegness is so Bracing' – well right now that's just a load of old puffery, the air's got a freshness about it sure, but it's a warm freshness, almost balmy. It's the week before Easter. I have to admit to be making a habit of bringing the kids to Butlins at this time of year. Even though you haven't asked I'll let you into a little secret – I come to Butlins for a thing called Spring Harvest. It's an annual gathering of Christians but it's not 'happy clappy' or cringe-making at all. The reason I keep coming back is that it's a lot of fun with great music, teaching, fellowship.... the only thing I can't stand is the plastic-coated mattress, it makes sleeping rather hazardous if you get my meaning.

I'm rather pleased with a couple of things that we've done already. First, one of the lads in our party celebrated his eleventh birthday and we all went ten-pin bowling. I was performing really poorly - I'd only scored 53 after seven frames which is deeply pathetic. With just three frames left I needed to do something miraculous to avoid coming last and losing what 'street cred' I'd managed to build by wearing a 'Billabong' turtle-neck sweater and carrying my son's skateboard around for him .

On a whim I ditched the 10-pound ball I'd been using and switched to a heavier one, one which would allow me to let the ball do the work. I can see myself stepping forward with renewed confidence, cradling the ball and then sliding it down the highly-polished bowling lane with just a little right hand side spin so that the ball thwacked into centre pin ever so slightly off centre. The pins shattered cleanly and went down as one – Crunch! A big 'X' appeared on the screen in front of me – 'Strike One'. On the ninth frame it was crunch all over again and the same on the tenth. I punched the air in glee - I'd struck 'Turkey' (for those not acquainted with the art of bowling that's a 'technical' term for three consecutive strikes) and it does wonders for your score. The turkey had landed, what a lovely Easter bird he was, and all because I'd let the ball do the work.

The other thing that had been really good was a trip out to a nearby nature reserve called Gibraltar Point. It's a well-known place for birdwatching just a few miles south of 'Skeggy' on a spit of land where the North Sea takes a chunk out of the east coast to form the amazing salty wilderness of The Wash. There were plenty of birds about but they paled into insignificance compared to the toads that were breeding in the dune slacks. They weren't just any old toads – these were natterjacks, a sort of smaller, wartier and rarer version of the amphibians we find skulking in dark and dank places in our gardens.

It seemed that every pool was full of toads. Toads resting. Toads mating. Toads suspended in crystal-clear water with no apparent purpose at all – like specimens preserved in the jars that line the walls of the Biology lab at school. Ugly – yes, very, but at the same time strangely beautiful and weird to see them suddenly move and evidence life. One pool was full of gelatinous spawn. It looked at first like a polluted froth but no, it was the beginning of new life, new life from out of a primeval swamp. So, what have turkeys and toads got to do with Kilimanjaro? I'm not sure right now. Perhaps I just like the alliteration!

"Hi, Mark. It's good to see you after so long. What can I get you?" I bring Mark's lager and my bitter back to a little table in a 'No Smoking' section of the pub. It's really quiet as everyone else is in the Big Top – that's the tent where I first heard about the Biscay Challenge last year, remember? We begin to chat against a wallpaper of sound – the throb of electric guitars, the occasional blast of a trumpet, the incessant rhythmic beat of an impressive percussion section and always the joyful sound of human voices singing songs of praise.

We get the usual pleasantries out of the way. Catch up on what's happened since we returned from the mountain. Trade notes on which climbers we've been in touch with and wonder, in particular, about how the guys from Zimbabwe are getting on. Then Mark poses the question I guess I'd been waiting for someone to ask for quite a while: "What did all we experience on that mountain really amount to?".

It got my mind going back to all the things I've already shared with you. The questioning of why I was doing it. The amazing experience of the climb itself, how it had seemed like a metaphor for our walk through this life with times when we feel like we can conquer the world and those when we just want to curl up and die. And, of course, the heartache of coming into close contact with scores of children under a death sentence from AIDS/HIV. It also made me focus on many other things. Things that happened once we'd left the National Park itself. The most powerful experiences occurred in the city of Arusha, one of the principal urban areas of Tanzania and the safari capital of the country as it lies adjacent to the great Serengeti, a Mecca for wildlife enthusiasts worldwide.

As third world cities go, Arusha might well be a really top class place, I don't know, as it's the only one I've visited. Compared to any European or American city I've ever been to it's dirt poor. When we went to exchange money we'd be swamped by hawkers trying to flog anything and everything: from Swahili phrase books to hunting spears, from sharp knives to intricate hardwood carvings. If our bus stopped in traffic for example, in a matter of seconds hawkers would descend on us again offering the same array of goods that I didn't want before and that I still didn't want.

I hated it. Hated it because I didn't like being hassled, didn't like my space being invaded. I also hated it because their very presence convicted me. It convicted me because I knew these people were desperate. They made me think things I didn't want to contemplate, made me face the fact that the decisions I made really could affect their lives in a dramatic way. Just one example illustrates how uncomfortable the whole thing was. A young woman tapped at the window as our bus stopped for some to take a comfort break. 'Jambo bwana' she mouthed through the glass. She held a bunch of bananas aloft and gradually swung it so that the yellowish green fruits, like fat little fingers, were right under my nose. As I recoiled, a question formed in my mind: 'If I don't buy these bananas, perhaps her kids won't eat tonight?'

I bought the bananas, not because I wanted to or needed them, but because I was convicted by that question. I felt guilty. I didn't feel better having bought them though, I felt worse, much worse. I hated having what they wanted but not wanting what they had to offer. Hated feeling that the question that convicted me might point to a false conclusion: that the woman wasn't really desperate and that I'd just been stung – another stupid tourist at the gateway to the wilderness. The odd thing was that when I ate some of the bananas I found them quite delicious – the nicest thing I'd eaten in days. Thinking about it now, seeing me sitting in our comfy bus chomping on those bananas I look for all the world like a great fat toad. Not a nice natterjack toad, I'm afraid. No! I'm one of those bloated, greedy things that we find in dark and dank places in our gardens.

I've spent what seems ages not answering Mark's question. I took a deep swig of my warm sweet beer. It felt very satisfying.

"The main thing it's amounted to is that it's changed my world-view, made me see that all my old priorities were just so wrong. Remember how as we approached the exit to the park kids started to appear asking for money and chocolate?"

I paused waiting for an answer but Mark was silent. "Well one of them came up to me with a great big branch on his head – firewood, I guess. It looked really heavy and he could only have been seven or eight years of age - about the same age as my youngest son. Although he was begging he was doing it with a lovely smile and I was mighty impressed with the way he was helping his parents out. Thinking about it that branch was nearly half a tree."

I paused again, still no comment from my fellow climber. "I knew we weren't supposed to give them anything – like they told us it only encourages them to beg and the tourists don't like it. But he just wouldn't give up. Eventually I took my rucksack off, hoping I'd have something suitable to give him so that he'd go on his way. All I could find was half a roll of loo paper and two one hundred dollar bills. To my shame I offered him the loo roll and he declined it. I'd like to think that, if I had my time again, I'd offer him one of the hundred dollar bills. Surely it would have made a bigger difference to him than some of the things I bought for myself have made for me"

I looked down and saw that both our glasses were empty. Mark made to get up but I put out my palm: "These are on me, same again?" He nodded and because we were virtually the only ones in the pub I got served straight away. As I waited for the pumps to deliver their measures I noticed the music for the first time since we'd first started chatting. The guy on the trumpet sounded like he was about to blow the top of his head off.

"Do you remember that bazaar we visited, the one we went to after we'd visited the woodcarving shop?" As I placed the refreshed glasses on the table a nod told me that it was remembered. "I've never felt more hated in my whole life than I did as we walked round that place. I keep thinking that my camera equipment was worth more than the contents of any of the stores. Don't get me wrong, it was a really interesting place - all those weird foodstuffs, colourful clothing and that mass of humanity - so full of characters!"

The guy on the trumpet was at it again forcing me to pause to recollect my thoughts. "The significance of that bazaar only struck me a few months later, you know. I was at this black tie business event. It was a tourism awards ceremony held in a banqueting suite next to a huge greenhouse full of tropical plants - a bit like the forest on the way up Kibo." Mark nodded and we both took swigs of ale. "Before the meal there was a drinks reception with a string quartet, or maybe it was a group of people in DJ's playing chamber music, I'm really not sure, but one thing's for certain it was a pretty upmarket event. I remember talking to someone there who owns a stately home and he'd had a pretty tough year as foot-and-mouth had meant he couldn't open to the public. Times had been hard for him.

"The main topic of conversation though was the World Trade Centre bombing. It was September 11th and the organiser's had very nearly cancelled as a mark of respect to the victims. At that time everyone was seized by a real fear. A fear that our western world was in peril. I know it sounds like 20:20 hindsight but I can honestly tell you, Mark, that I wasn't surprised. I was horrified by the pictures we'd all seen on the TV before we'd left for the dinner, but I wasn't surprised because I could remember the atmosphere in that bazaar. I could hear the reggae music, the chanted lyrics of protest and I understood the hatred I had felt much better. I recognised that there's still a really fertile ground for evil people to encourage ordinary people to want to get their revenge. I'm not saying it justifies, but I could imagine a terrorist leader walking up to that little kid in ten years time and saying: 'the West say they help us but what have they ever done for you?' And his answer: 'Someone once offered me half a loo roll'."

The glasses were empty again but neither of us felt like more drink. It was good to have been asked that question but although climbing the mountain has changed me, what good will it do? I've been pondering that question ever since I got back from Skegness on Maundy Thursday. So my world-view has changed, maybe I did see the light on Kibo but what can I do about all the suffering I saw, what can any of us do? On one level I think the answer is that we need to do whatever it is that we feel we can. Any action, however small, makes a difference and surely big differences are often made by an accumulation of little things. You climb a great mountain slowly, slowly, with lots of small steps none of which seems significant but each of which carries you towards the peak.

On another level though, I'm not so sure that we can ever create a heaven on earth. Getting to the top of the great mountain was a really wonderful, emotional experience for all of us, but it was so hard and once we'd got there we just had to come straight down again like a Newtonian apple. It was the mountain that conquered us, although it did give us a glimpse of something special. It's not for me to say whether freedom's been a good thing for Tanzania but it certainly hasn't been a panacea. That's something of which I'm sure. So what is the answer?

Photo: DC

On Easter Sunday I went to church. I've got the programme in front of me right now and on the front page it says in big lettering: 'He is risen, Alleluia!'. Beneath these words in much smaller type there's a quote from the Bible:

'For God, who said, "Let light shine out of darkness," made his light shine in our hearts to give us the light of the knowledge of the glory of God in the face of Christ.'
2 Cor 4:6

They are the very words that inspired the artist who made a stained glass window for the church to mark the new millennium. When the light shines through it, it's as though there's this tiny cross in the heart of a sea of trouble and yet, somehow, you know that the cross will win. Maybe all we have to do, even though it's easier said than done, is to recognise that Christ has already done the real work. And we've just got to do our bit as individuals.

Epilogue

I asked several of my fellow climbers for their thoughts on our experiences, and two of them, James Collis from London and Mark Beniston from Leicester had this to say:

First James Collis:

'When I applied to climb Kilimanjaro I was fairly confident. As an almost fit (and slightly over ambitious twenty one year old) I could not see the struggle ahead. I'd climbed up to Annapurna base camp in Nepal at around 4400 metres without using any real climbing equipment or common sense. Kilimanjaro at 5895 metres didn't seem much more of a struggle. It seemed like the perfect holiday. Raising money for charity and doing something a bit different.

'As we took off from Birmingham Airport I was filled with a sense of happiness and anticipation. The first night driving through the Tanzanian outback overwhelmed me. Straight away the realization of what we were about to embark on was showing on every face as we moved ever on into the night, and we had still not seen the mountain. The next day the mountain showed its awesome peaks and it became obvious to us all – this was not going to be easy.

'Over the coming days we all learnt a lot about ourselves and each other. Walking for eight to ten hours most days was hard work. The higher we got the thinner the air became. Flora and fauna changed every day without fail. It was the most beautiful yet painful time any of us could remember, and the higher we walked the more awe-inspired we became.

'The final assault on the mountain was as hard and arduous as we had been promised and then some! Not one person on our climb found it a hurdle that was easy to pass. As we hit the top our hearts were filled with joy and relief. We said a prayer and I looked around and admired the beauty of God's creation. The cold wind and rising sun became too much – I was literally overawed.'

And now Mark Beniston:

'It wasn't until the sun rose that it really struck me. Seeing poverty live on the TV or even picturing it in my mind hadn't prepared me for what stared me right in the face before we began the climb. The biggest challenge for me turned out to be coming to terms with my own conscience, and I had a good few days on a huge, lonely mountain to do just that.

'Maintaining eye contact with a young child who has AIDS, half a set of clothes and his hand held out for absolutely anything you might give him - hoping that on a whim you might be generous enough to save his life for another day - is, without doubt, the hardest thing I've ever been confronted with. Of course, giving him my portion of food or money may not necessarily be doing him any favours. But being an innocent child he must wonder why a 'rich man' would not give something to him — unless that man was some kind of inhumane monster. And why on earth would that rich man cry?

'Unlike watching the TV, anyone who actually visits a developing country is directly confronted with the opportunity to help that poor, innocent, crying kid that needs their help. And the hundreds more they're likely to meet rushing out of their houses to collect what they can. Since the word most commonly used for 'white man' in Swahili is the same as the word used for 'money', I suspect that were any westerner to give away all their possessions and walk through a village naked they would still be expected to help (or save) them via wealth.

'I can't possibly blame them for my guilt, I must simply struggle in my own mind to come to terms with how such an abomination of life, by any moral standard, is allowed to exist in a world of plenty and why it has for so long! 'Blessed are the poor' is often a baffling statement to the westerner, and usually no substitute for wealth to the average African. It's clear that wealth does provide too much room for corruption in the human heart. Should the world's resources be shared more equally there might be a lot less in the way of pollution and weaponry, and poverty probably wouldn't exist at all.

'The Kilimanjaro challenge got me to Africa and enabled me to raise money for a good cause. On that mountain I saw some of the most beautiful sights I shall perhaps ever see in this life. It's strange to contrast that with what I saw when I wasn't climbing – with the three days either side.

'It's been said before but I think the challenge we all face is what should we do about Africa?'

The Story of a Trek Files

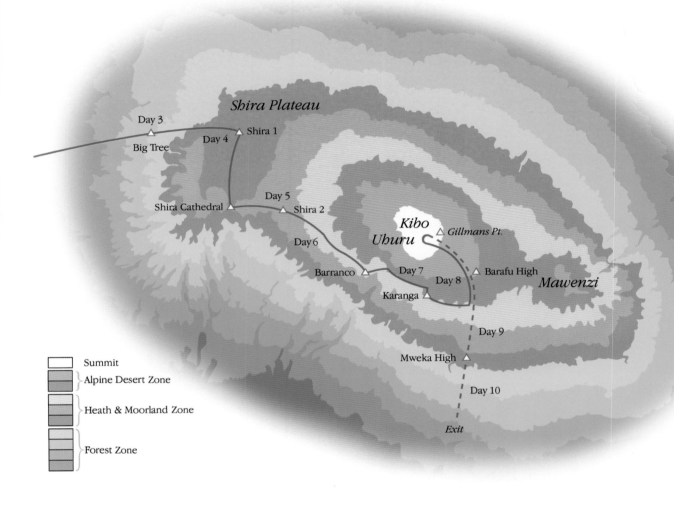

Shira Plateau

Day 3
△
Big Tree

Day 4
△ Shira 1

Shira Cathedral △

Day 5
△ Shira 2

Kibo
Uhuru
△ Gillmans Pt.

Day 6

Barranco △

Day 7
Day 8
△ Barafu High

Mawenzi

Karanga △

Day 9

Mweka High △

Day 10

Exit

☐ Summit
Alpine Desert Zone

Heath & Moorland Zone

Forest Zone

Indicative only.

The Trek File

Day 1

Early morning flight from Birmingham to Amsterdam and onto Kilimanjaro. Arrive approx 2100hrs local time for the transfer to a hotel in Moshi (just outside Arusha) for a light supper and overnight stay.

Day 2

After the long journey from the night before, you can enjoy a relaxing day to acclimatize to your new surroundings.

Day 3

After orientation and kit check, register at Londorossi Gate. Then drive to road head near Lemosho Glades and start the trek through the rain forest, camp near Big Tree (9170ft/2750mts). This is an exciting wilderness route. It is being used to avoid potential overcrowding on the Machame Route and to take the climbers to true wilderness zones. Three of the camps are sites recently established. Our trek this day will be along a little used track known as Chamber's route. In places the vegetation is so undisturbed by humans that it grows right across the narrow track. Flora and fauna are richer here than on more popular routes through the rain forest.

Day 4

A full day's trek with a height gain of over 2000ft/600mts, taking us to a lunch stop at a beautiful valley just outside the Shira Crater at around 10000ft/3050mts. After lunch we cross into the Shira Caldera, a high altitude desert plateau rarely visited by man. Shira is the third of Kilimanjaro's volcanic cones. It is both filled with lava flow from Kibo and its rim eroded and blasted away by weather and volcanic action. Camp at Shira One (11500ft/3500mts) This day expect the first close views of Kibo – the dramatic summit cone of Kilimanjaro.

Day 5

Early morning start for acclimatizing trek to Shira Cathedral. The views from the top of this ridge are very special. Those with vertigo should take care. Trek across Shira Plateau to our camp which is located at around 12200ft/3700mts.

Day 6

A superb day's trekking that takes us to the southern flank, passing down the Barranco Valley to the camp at Barranco Wall. Here we camp at 12900ft/3940mts not much higher than our camp at Shira; but the walk will have taken us well over 15000ft/4570mts offering valuable altitude acclimatization. The camp at Barranco is one of the most spectacular on Kilimanjaro.

Day 7

Early morning climb up Barranco Wall (14000ft/4270mts with a height gain of 700ft steep and 300ft east ascent) to admire the views of Meru and the plains far below. Then continue across the ridges and valleys to Karanga valley. Optional and highly useful acclimatization trek to visit the first ice and try scree walking.

Day 8

Early start to reach our new Barafu Ridge high camp (16000ft/4600mts). The trek up Barafu Ridge is tough because of the altitude. We bypass Barafu Hut (standard camp) and continue one and a half hours to the higher camp zone. This gives you optimum acclimatization, and makes the trek to the summit later this night a good deal shorter. Dinner will be early with an afternoon sleep to rest before the summit trek.

Day 9

Rise around midnight to commence the trek up scree slopes to Stella Point on the rim. We should reach this point at dawn and then continue around the rim to the highest point – Uhuru Point. A few precious moments to enjoy the amazing views before we return to Stella Point and descend the scree via Barafu Ridge to our new Mweka route high camp 11500/3500mts).

This is to be the toughest day that most trekkers have ever experienced, involving 3600ft/1100mts of ascent, 7200ft/2200mts descent, and 12 to 15 hours walking. It is victory day.

Day 10

Walk down across the moorland to Mweka Hut and onto Mweka Gate for picnic, presentation of certificates and photos. Please note that this is a tough half day trek especially if there is rain on the route. Stepping over large tree roots and clambering down mud runnels is hard on tired limbs. Nevertheless, the route is very beautiful and worth the effort. After a picnic lunch drive to a Moshi hotel for a welcome shower, dinner and overnight stay.

Day 11

The morning can be spent at leisure and in the afternoon you will transfer to Kilimanjaro International Airport for your homeward bound flight to Birmingham via Amsterdam.

Day 12

Arrive back at Birmingham.

Tanzania File

Area	945,087 square Kilometres
Population	20 million
Capital	Dodoma, although Arusha is known as the Safari capital of the north and Dar es Salaam is the administrative capital.
Language	English and Swahili although there are over 100 tribal dialects.
Tipping	A good supply of $1 bills helps with tipping.
Time	Three hours ahead of GMT.
Photography	Do not take photos of anything connected with the government or the military (government offices, post offices, bridges, railway stations etc). You may well be arrested and your film will be confiscated.
Currency	Tanzania Shilling

Currency Regulations	The Tanzania shilling is a soft currency and you cannot obtain them before leaving the UK. However, US dollars are accepted in most places.
Vaccinations	Yellow Fever – essential . Recommended - Typhoid, Hepatitis A&B, Diptheria, Rabies, Meningitis, Polio, Tetanus & Malaria.
Risks	You must wear long sleeves and trousers at dawn and at dusk. An insect repellent must also be carried with you at all times. You must ensure you have adequate precautions against malaria. There is a high prevalence of AIDS/HIV
Water	Water must be sterilised (boiled and filtered or bought in brand bottles). Avoid drinks containing ice. Remember not to swim in rivers and lakes.
Climate	Tanzania's widely varying geography accounts for its variety of climatic conditions. The climate is tropical or temperate rather than equatorial. There are minimal temperature changes throughout the year. Inland temperatures are around 25 degrees C. Coastal areas are hot and humid with an average day temperature of 30 degrees C. Monsoon winds bring most of the country's rain. The long rains are from March to May with occasional rain between October and December.

Geography	A land of plains, lakes and mountains with a narrow coastal belt, Tanzania is East Africa's largest country. The bulk of its 945,087 sq.km is a highland plateau, some of it desert or semi-desert and the rest savannah and scattered bush.
History	Not a great deal is known about the early history the Tanzanian interior except that by 1800 AD, the Masai, who in previous centuries had grazed their cattle in the Lake Turkana region of Kenya, had migrated down the rift valley as far as Dodoma. Their advance was only stopped by the Gogo, who occupied an area west of the Rift Valley, and the Hehe to the south of Dodoma. Because of their reputation as a warrior tribe, the Masai were feared by the neighbouring Bantu tribes and avoided by the Arab traders. Due to this, the northern part of Tanzania was almost free from the depredations of the slave trade and the civil wars that detroyed so many villages and settlements in other areas of the country.
	Zanzibar and Tanganyika merged in 1964 to form the United Republic of Tanzania.
Culture/Customs	Variations are enormous because of the number of tribes. The 50:50 Muslim:Christian divide does create basic religious differences.

Health File

General Precautions

Visitors to the tropics are prone to dehydration and heat related conditions. This is particularly so in the first few days of travel and more so if the traveller is exerting him or herself, e.g. trekking. Drink a lot more non-alcoholic liquid than normal and increase your intake of ordinary table salt. About two extra teaspoons of salt per person per day is a rough guide. Simply put more on your food. Do not bother with salt tablets as they are not easily absorbed by the body. Cover up with light, loose fitting clothing and use a good sun block on any exposed skin. Always wear a wide sun hat and ensure your neck is covered.

Drinking water, including water for cleaning your teeth, must be pure. Boil for at least four minutes, filter, or use iodine or chlorine tablets.

Personal hygiene is most important; and you should wash hands thoroughly before eating and after using the toilet. Scrub with a nailbrush and soap for around three minutes. Baby wipes and antiseptic wipes are very useful and you should always have some in your daypack.

Avoid petting any animals.

Avoid being bitten by insects particularly the mosquito. Avoid malaria by avoiding being bitten and by taking regularly the tablets prescribed by your GP.

Treat even small wounds and scratches urgently. Abrasions in the tropics are most likely to become infected. Clean the wound and dress it. Change the dressing regularly.

Trekking and Expeditions

Hot and dusty conditions can lead to fluid loss, salt loss and overheating of the body. This can cause heat exhaustion or even heat stroke. In heat exhaustion symptoms are profuse sweating, dizziness and fatigue. Treatment consists of removing the patient from the sun, fanning or cool sponging and oral re-hydration. Heat stroke is a potentially fatal condition and differs from heat exhaustion in that the body temperature rises above 40 degrees centigrade. Sweating may cease, the body will be very hot to touch, headache is likely along with mental disturbance. Urgent treatment to remove the patient from the sun, surface cool the body with cool liquid followed by evacuation to hospital. Other physical conditions likely to occur are sunburn and dust/grit in the eyes. Cover exposed skin, use sun block and wear sunglasses. If a contact lens wearer it may be advisable to take a pair of spectacles.

Good footwear and care of feet is most important. Well broken in walking boots should be worn. Trainers are too flimsy for wilderness treks. Sandals leave the feet exposed to sunburn, abrasions, thorns, insect and animal bites. Any soreness of the feet should be treated immediately with 'second skins' or other dressings. Treating sores early will help avoid crippling problems developing later. It is better to hold up the group for a few minutes to apply an initial dressing rather than to handicap the expedition with serious lameness caused by untreated sores.

Impact of High Altitude on the Human Body and Brain

- As altitude increases barometric pressure (a measure of the 'weight' of air) reduces.

- At 19000 feet barometric pressure is half that of sea level.

- As a direct result of this fall in pressure, oxygenation decreases.

- In July/August atmospheric pressure is universally higher than other times of the year. It is therefore better to be climbing at the equator in mid summer.

Hypoxia (the reduction of oxygen content) may lead to :

- AMS (Acute Mountain Sickness)

- HAPE (High Altitude Pulmonary Oedema or fluid in the lungs), and

- HACE (High Altitude Cerebral Oedema or fluid on the brain).

To avoid these conditions it is best to acclimatise to the increasing altitude by climbing slowly. It is possible to use a regime of drugs such as Diamox to deter AMS and the more serious HAPE & HACE.

AMS: normally develops about 6 – 12 hours after critical altitude is reached. Serious effects of altitude have been documented as low as 3000 feet; but in most cases problems will materialise around 12000 feet. A height gain of around 1000 feet per day with a rest day after every 3000 feet is ideal for most people to acclimatise successfully. Virtually all climbers will experience some of the symptoms of AMS although in a sense AMS can be thought of as a relatively benign condition that could lead to the more serious conditions of HAPE & HACE. AMS symptoms are some or all of the following and are likely to be found in the following % of cases: headache (96%), sleep disturbed (70%), loss of appetite (38%), nausea (35%), dizziness and lasitude (27%) and vomiting (14%).

Prevention and reduction of AMS: climb slowly, discuss with your doctor a drug regime such as Diamox, and be very fit. Fit climbers are 17% likely to suffer, whereas unfit climbers are 43% likely to suffer. AMS need not lead to the abandonment of a climb. If the symptoms are mild a rest day at the same or a lower altitude may be sufficient.

However, if the symptoms persist the climber must descend. Otherwise there is the real risk that the illness will develop into the more serious and life-threatening HAPE or HACE.

HAPE: symptoms (some similar to AMS) demand immediate descent or death may result. They include: breathlessness on exertion, cough, breathlessness at rest, gurgling in the chest, blood in sputum. One of the first symptoms is more than average breathlessness on climbing, followed by breathlessness at rest, often accompanied by a cough. Immediate descent is required and (if possible) a drug regime of Nifedipine.

HACE: usually occurs only above 12000 feet and after rapid ascent. The incidence in the Himalayas is 2% of climbers going to above 13200 feet. Symptoms generally, but not always, seem like those of AMS but the headache is severe and not relieved by analgesics. Further symptoms may include: vertigo, ataxia (unsteady movements and balance), and hallucinations. As ataxia is usually one of the first symptoms to appear it is worth doing a heel to toe walking test. Treatment is descent and more descent. Drug regime of Dexamethasone may help.

Further Conditions associated with High Altitude

Eyes: retinal haemorrhages are common and, if they appear to enlargen, descent is advised. Snow blindness caused by UV light damaging the cornea.

Gastro-Intestinal System: is affected and weight loss is to be expected. On a 3-6 week expedition to altitudes over 12000 feet climbers can expect to lose 12 to 17lbs. Climbers lose most weight during the first few days at altitude. We consume more energy at altitude and the fall in temperature demands an increase in diet. Furthermore our basal metabolic rate increases in spite of the good clothing and protective gear. Overall expect to need about 450kcal/day extra.

Dehydration is possible and liquid intake should be kept up. But there is no evidence that lots of liquid prevents AMS. Hypoxia stimulates a urine flow. The conclusion seems to be: 'drink more than usual, but not to the point of nausea'.

The skin at altitude is at risk from the increased UV, the cold and the wind. Symptoms include: ageing, sunburn, cold sores, prickly heat and UV conjuctivitis.

Peripheral Oedema or swelling of hands and feet is sometimes noted at altitude. The symptoms usually diminish after a few days and they do not necessarily herald HACE or HAPE.

Hypothermia arises when the body core temperature is caused to drop to between 35 and 32 degrees centigrade. Symptoms include shivering, stumbling and poor co-ordination. Treatment includes: warm dry clothes, warm packs and plenty to drink. Below 32 degrees is considered to be severe hypothermia and when the core temperature falls below 30 degrees shivering will cease. The patient must be disturbed as little as possible, insulated with warm items such as a sleeping bag, and very gently taken to a lower altitude. This is a very serious condition requiring skilled medical attention.

Kilimanjaro File

Nomenclature

The name 'Kilimanjaro' is a hugely romantic and evocative one, but where it originates from is largely a matter of conjecture. Theories abound, but it is widely held that the name is probably a Chagga (the third largest ethnic group in Tanzania whose homeland is on the lower slopes of Kilimanjaro), Masai or Swahili name, or a combination of the three. Kilimanjaro may mean 'mountain of of greatness', 'mountain of water', or 'white mountain' or various other interpretations including the name of a demon held to live in the mountain who creates cold.

The origin of the names of Kilimanjaro's two big peaks is more straightforward. Kibo (kippoo) means 'spotted' in Chagga in reference to the rock and snow mix. Mawenzi is Chagga for 'broken top'.

Vital Statistics

Kilimanjaro is the highest point of Africa and one of the highest free standing mountains in the world. It consists of three extinct or dormant volcanoes:

Kibo: 5895 metres
Mawenzi: 5149 metres
Shira: 3962 metres

Kilimanjaro rises 4800 metres from the plains and at its widest is 40km across.

Most of a volcano's mass is hidden from sight, we can see only a hundredth or even just a thousandth part. They can be regarded as tiny pin pricks on the earth's crust through which molten lava and gas may be released.

There are just 20sq.km of glaciers on the whole African continent and Kilimanjaro boasts one-fifth of this amount.

Geological origins can be traced back to the formation of the Great Rift Valley which stretches from the Red Sea beyond Tanzania deep into the heart of Africa. The valley was formed relatively recently in geological terms – some 1 to 2 million years ago.

Kilimanjaro is 330km south of the equator.

History

Research has indicated that the area of Kilimanjaro was inhabitated at the birth of Christ. The first written reference to the great mountain is however, believed to have been made by Ptolemy some 18 centuries ago. In modern times the mountain was immortalised by the American writer Ernest Hemmingway and the mysterious 'white-leopard'.

The mountain was not revealed to the West until an article written by a Swiss German missionary named Johannes Rebmann appeared in the Church Missionary Intelligencer in April 1849. Many didn't believe his account. It took a dozen years for what he recounted to be widely accepted as the truth.

Another missionary, Charles New, made a serious attempt to conquer Kilimanjaro in 1871 but drew back at the snowline (about 4000 metres/13,200 feet)

On 5th October 1889 Kilimanjaro was conquered for the first time by Dr Hans Meyer and his colleague Ludwig Purtscheller. They named the summit Kaiser Wilhelm Spitze.

Contrary to popular rumour, Kilimanjaro is not in Tanzania because it was given as a birthday present by Queen Victoria to her grandson (the future Kaiser Wilhelm) to compensate for Germany not having a snow-capped mountain in its empire!

Ecology

It is widely recognised that there are five distinct ecological zones within the area known as 'Kilimanjaro' – the lower slopes, forest, heath and moorland, highland desert and the summit. Each zone is distinctive in terms of its animal and plant life which is governed by a combination of altitude, rainfall and temperature.

Each zone spans some 1000m from the bottom of the volcano to the summit. The temperature drops by approximately 1 degree centigrade every 200m as one climbs upwards.

Subscribers

Grace Publishing Ltd; thanks the following individuals and organisations who through their generosity and support have made the publication of this book possible. Their names are listed here in alphabetical order in grateful recognition. However, the views expressed in 'A Candle on Kilimanjaro' are those of the author alone and subscribers do not necessarily endorse them in whole or in part.

Jerry Allen	Dorridge
Zoë Almond	Stratford-upon-Avon
Neil Anderson	Birmingham
The Anderson Family	Langley
Bert & Molly Anderson	Broughty Ferry
Anthony & Helen Archer	Claverdon
Dr David & Nicky Arnott	Claverdon
Shona & Ian Bates	Alvechurch
Andrew Beckett	Warwick
Maggie Bellamy	West Sussex
Mark Beniston	Leicestershire
Sue Brown	Bewdley
Roy & Sheila Bryant	Essex
Catherine Freeman	Leicester
David & Ruth Burman	Claverdon

David Clark	Warwickshire
Neil Clarke & Joy Arthur	Long Marston
H J Clarke	Claverdon
Les & Ann Clayton	Warwickshire
Ian Clayton	Staffordshire
Bernard & Gloria Close	Henley-in-Arden
James Collis	London
Mr & Mrs W. Collis	Ilfracombe
Mr & Mrs W. Collis	London
David Cooper	Birmingham
Pat Couchman	Studley
Pete Cullen	Coventry
Neill Currie	Coventry
Alan & Nicola Dean	Worcestershire
Sam Diah	Tanzania
Alan & Lorna Dick	Balsall Common
David Dixie	Birmingham
John Dobson	Norton Canes
Stan Donaghy	Long Whatton
Joan Donegan	Redditch
Michael Downey & Jean Darr	Worcester
Susan Dunbar	Hockley Heath
Charles Eid	Dunstable

Ivor Elcock	Lichfield
Josie Elt	Barnstaple
Jonathan & Gill Evans	Claverdon
Jean Elwell	Sedgley
Felix	Tanzania
Rob Fielding	Dudley
Trisha Finnemore	Birmingham
Dr Colin Flenley	Walsall
Mrs P Fletcher	Wolverhampton
Carol Follis	Sutton Coldfield
Sara Fookes	Gloucester
Don Foster	Stratford-upon-Avon
Susan Freeborough	Bishops Tachbrook
Mike & Sandra Freeman	Dudley
Mrs Lois Freeman	Lincoln
Nathanel Freeman	RAF Waddington
Nick Gainsford	Dudley
Brent Garner	Stratford-upon-Avon
Gill & Richard	Lincolnshire
Carrol Geake	Wiltshire
Rev. Dr. Michael Green	Oxford
Annabelle Guyver	Mickleton
Phil & Penny Hanson	Claverdon

Samuel Harkin	Birmingham
Emma Herridge	London
Barbara Holden	Solihull
Bryan Holden	Solihull
Alex Holden	Henley-in-Arden
Beth Holden	Henley-in-Arden
Doug Holden	Henley-in-Arden
Lisa & Craig Holden	Harborne
David Holker	Nuneaton
Sue Hollingsworth	Claverdon
Natalie Hopper	Newton le Willows
Mr & Mrs R Horsmann	Worcester
Paul & Diana Hunt	Claverdon
Iain & Heather Inglis	Uddingston
Kevin & Jenny Herbert	Daventry
Rachel James	Costa Rica
Joachim	Tanzania
John Johnson	Henley-in-Arden
Thomas E Jones	Sedgley
Charles & Jan Keil	Solihull
John and Val Lambert	Claverdon
Andrew Leigh	Solihull
Jane Leigh	Solihull

Liz & Simon	Borehamwood
Marilyn & Dave	Lincoln
David Marsh	Droitwich
Andy Marshall	Derbyshire
Gail Mattocks	Cradley Heath
Jan Millar	Warwickshire
Averil & Gregg Millar	Warwickshire
Sarah Montgomery	Hanbury
Norrie Moore	Hatton
Gill Morgan	Knowle
Tony & Carolyn Morgan	Henley-in-Arden
Brian & Liz Ollis	Claverdon
Roy & Linda Osborne	Redditch
Steve Parker-Brown	Warwickshire
Ian Pegg	Lancashire
Nicola Pickering	New Oscott
Janet Pinn	Warwickshire
Dave Pope	Dudley
Julie Price	Shropshire
Michael Priddis	Warwickshire
The Ritchie Family	Hockley Heath
Barbara Sallows	Redditch
Carol Savage	Claverdon

Julia Seymour-Smith	Snitterfield
Hugh Scurfield	Shropshire
Sharon & Bob	Lincolnshire
Chris, Elaine, Stuart, Imogen & Ewan Shelley	Bristol
Allan & Anne Smillie	Giffnock
Peter Slater	Wheathampstead
Andrew Sparrow	Birmingham
Spring Parker Brown	Hockley Heath
The Steel Family	Nailsea
Rev. Dr. Chris Sugden	Oxford
John Swinburne	Knowle
Cathy Szary	Scunthrope
Laura Taylor & Family	Claverdon
Carol Thompson	Gloucester
Peter Townley	Eckington
Rafael Vargas	Costa Rica
Vera Wilkes	Sedgley
Jackie & David Ward	Wolverhampton
Pauline Westwood	Alcester
Alma Westwood	Bromsgrove
Neil Willies	Broom
Ian Willis	Langley
Graham Wright	Wolverhampton
Sue Wright	Henley-in-Arden

The '2001 Kilimanjaro Challenge' was organised by Trailblazers, a project of the Saltmine Trust.

Trailblazers operates a programme of challenges with the intention of raising funds from sponsorship in support of worldwide humanitarian aid projects. The range of challenges currently includes:

Fastnet Sailing Challenge
Biscay Sailing Challenge
Great Wall of China Trek

Mongolian Trek
Mt Cotopaxi
Mt Kilimanjaro

Projects supported include:

Care For The Family – UK
Plymouth City Mission – UK
Langley House Trust – UK
Saltmine Trust
Christian Aid Trust
Oasis India – Mumbai

Tonga Tribe Water Project – Zimbabwe
Toybox Charity – Guatemala
Bethany Children's Trust – Mozambique
Tigers Club – Uganda
Arab World Ministries

For more information view: www.saltmine.org/trailblazers

Mike Freeman, MBE, who led the 2001 Kilimanjaro Challenge is now Director of The Right Hand Trust. The Trust is a registered charity that offers a life enriching 'Gap Year Challenge' for 18-30yr olds. The first six months are spent in the UK training and preparing for an eight month assignment in Africa. Participants will serve others in a rural village in Christian parishes in one of several different countries. Conditions are often basic with water possibly coming from a communal standpipe and the toilet a hole in the ground!

For more information view: www.righthandtrust.org.uk